WITH A CD OF PIANO ACCOMPANIMENTS

LOW VOICE

THE STUDENT SINGER

25 SONGS IN ENGLISH
for CLASSICAL VOICE

EDITED BY
RICHARD WALTERS

ISBN 978-1-4584-1125-9

HAL•LEONARD®
CORPORATION
7777 W. BLUEMOUND RD. P.O. BOX 13819 MILWAUKEE, WI 53213

Visit Hal Leonard Online at
www.halleonard.com

CONTENTS BY SONG

PIANISTS ON THE CD:

Catherine Bringerud (Track 18)

Christopher Ruck (Track 23)

Richard Walters (Tracks 5-8, 12, 14, 21)

Laura Ward (Tracks 1-4, 9-11, 13, 15-17, 19, 20, 22, 24, 25)

CONTENTS BY GENRE

Page   Piano Accompaniment
CD Track No.

ART SONGS

FOLKSONG ARRANGEMENTS

All Through the Night

Welsh folksong
arranged by Nicholl

Bright is the ring of words

from *Songs of Travel*

Robert Louis Stevenson
(1850–1894)

Ralph Vaughan Williams
(1872–1958)

wings they are car - ried– Af - ter the sing - er is

dead And the mak - er bur - ied._____ Low as the

sing - er lies_____ In the field of heath - er, Songs of his

fash - ion bring The swains to - geth - er.

The Call

from *Five Mystical Songs*

George Herbert
(1593–1633)

Ralph Vaughan Williams
(1872–1958)

Lento moderato

Come, my Way, my Truth, _ my Life: Such a

Way, as gives _ us breath: Such a Truth, as ends all strife: Such a

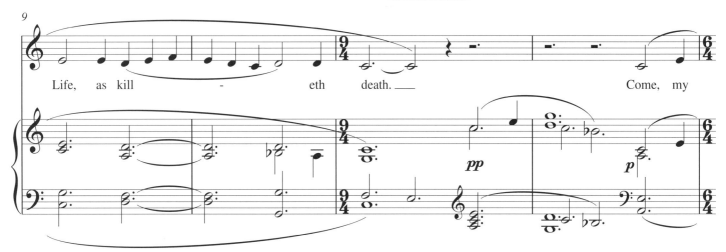

Life, as kill - eth death. _ Come, my

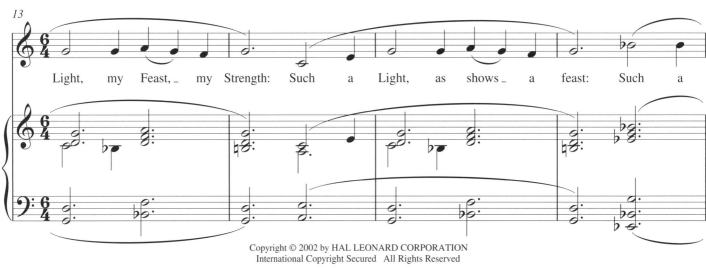

Light, my Feast, _ my Strength: Such a Light, as shows _ a feast: Such a

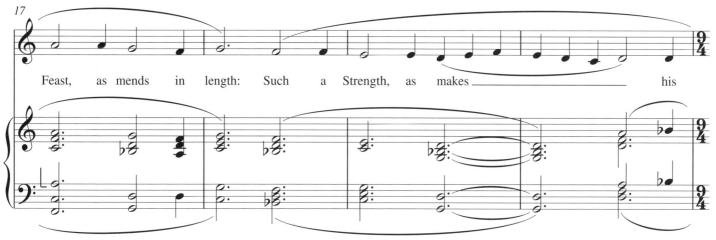

Feast, as mends in length: Such a Strength, as makes _____ his

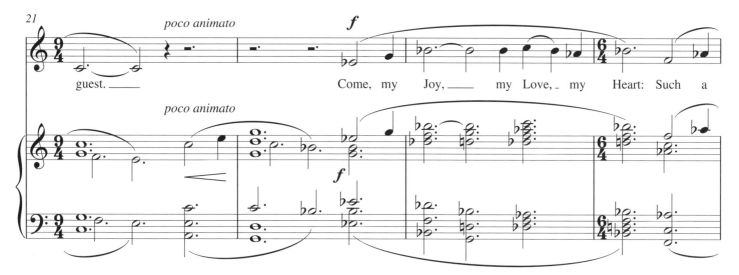

guest. _____ Come, my Joy, _____ my Love, _____ my Heart: Such a

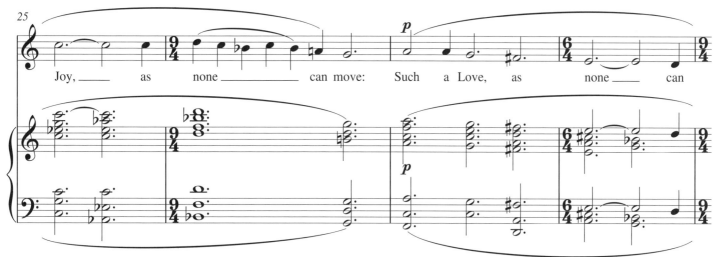

Joy, _____ as none _____ can move: Such a Love, as none _____ can

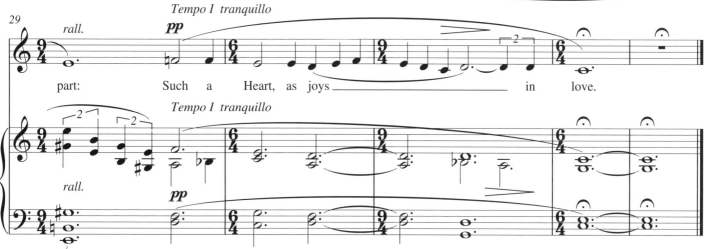

part: Such a Heart, as joys _____ in love.

Come again, sweet love

Anonymous

John Dowland
(1563–1626)
realized by Richard Walters

*Small size notes are optional for verse two.

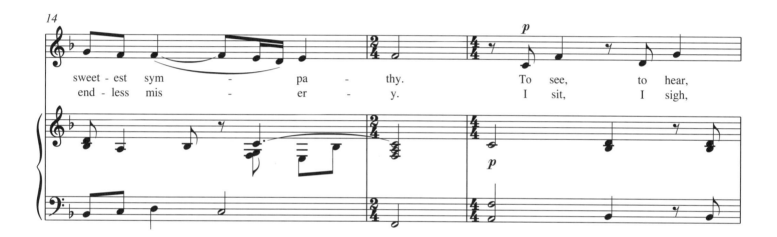

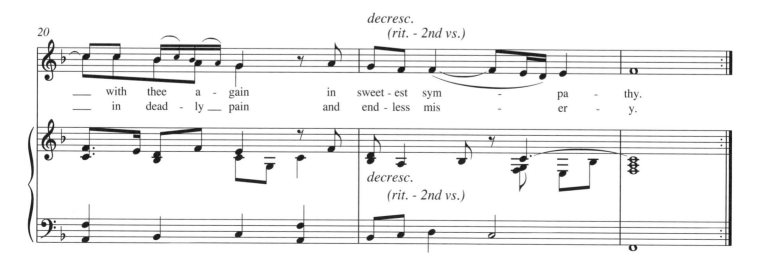

The Gospel Train

African-American Spiritual
arranged by Richard Walters

board, lit - tle chil - dren, get on board, lit - tle

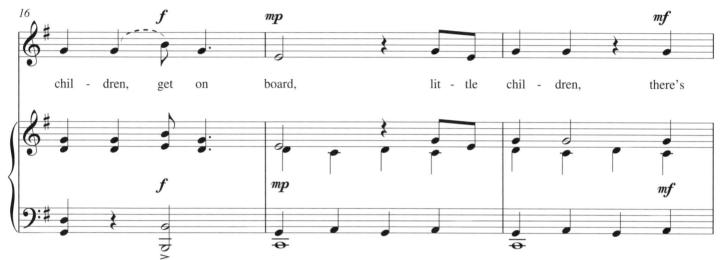

chil - dren, get on board, lit - tle chil - dren, there's

room for man - y a - more. The

fare is cheap and __ all can go, __ the rich and poor are

there. _ No sec - ond class _ a - board this train, no

dif - f'rence in the fare. ___ Oh, get on board, lit - tle

chil - dren, get on board, lit - tle chil - dren, get on board, lit - tle

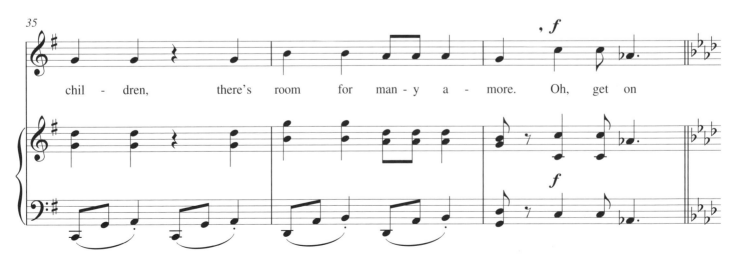

chil - dren, there's room for man - y a - more. Oh, get on

board, lit - tle chil - dren, get on board, lit - tle

chil - dren, get on board, lit - tle chil - dren, there's

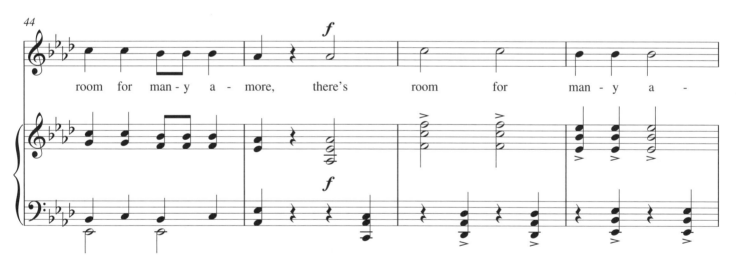

room for man - y a - more, there's room for man - y a -

more.

Greensleeves

16th century English Folksong
arranged by Bryan Stanley

Andante con moto ♩ = 50-58

1. A -

las, my love, _____ you do me wrong to
vows my you've bro - ken, do like me my heart, Oh,

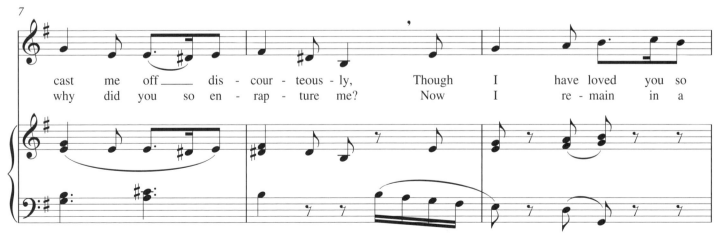

cast me off _____ dis - cour - teous - ly, Though I have loved you so
why did you so en - rap - ture me? Now I re - main in a

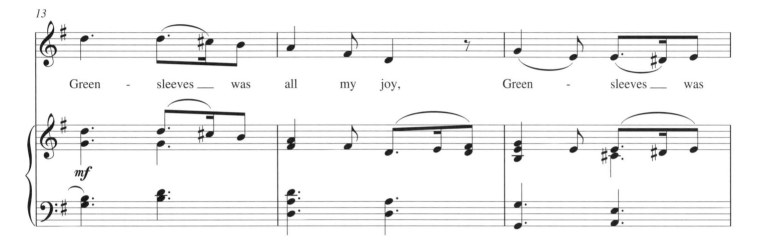

Green - sleeves?   3. I

with pedal

have   been   read   -   y   at   your   hand   to

grant   what - ev - er   you   would crave.   I   have   both   wa - gered

life   and   land,   Your   love   and good will   for   to   have.

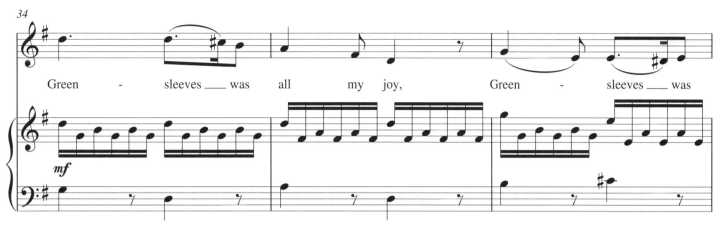

Green - sleeves ___ was all my joy, Green - sleeves ___ was

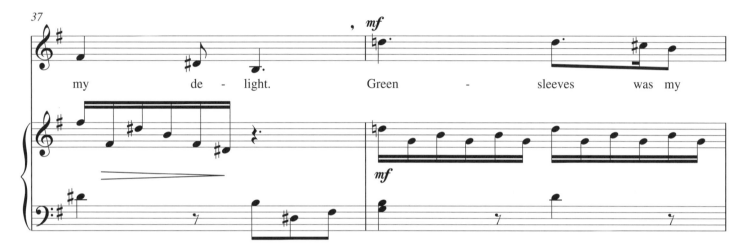

my de - light. Green - sleeves was my

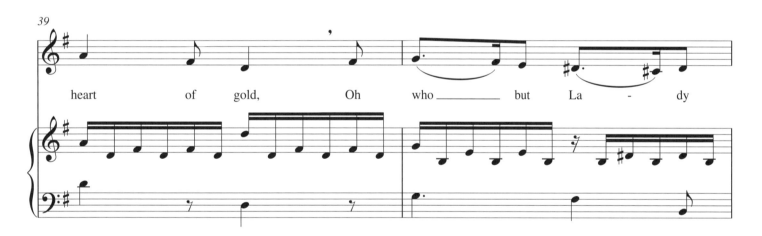

heart of gold, Oh who ___ but La - dy

Green - sleeves? Who ___ but La - dy Green - sleeves?

He's Got the Whole World in His Hands

African-American Spiritual
arranged by Joel K. Boyd

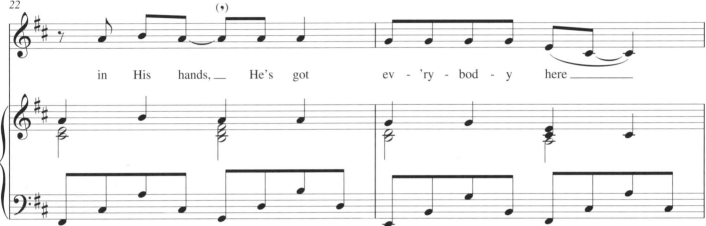

5. He's got the whole world _____ in His hands, _ He's got the

whole wide world _____ in His hands, _ He's got the

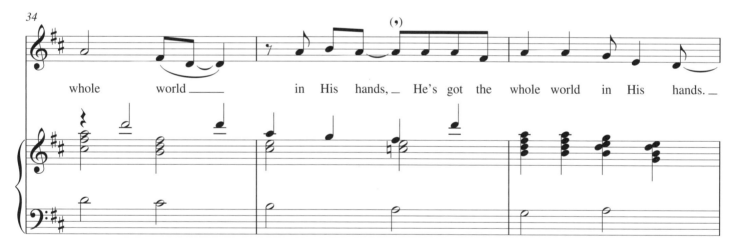

whole world _____ in His hands, _ He's got the whole world in His hands. _

He's got the whole world in His hands. _

How Can I Keep from Singing

Words possibly by
Anna Bartlett Warner
(1827–1915)

American Tune
Music possibly by
Robert Wadsworth Lowry
(1826–1899)
arranged by Christopher Ruck

1. My life flows on in
though the tem - pest

end - less song a - bove earth's lam - en - ta - tion. I
'round me rears, I know the truth, it liv - eth. What

hear the real, though far off hymn that hails a new cre -
though the dark - ness 'round me close, Songs in the nights it

a - tion. No storm can shake my in - most calm while
giv - eth. No storm can shake my in - most calm while

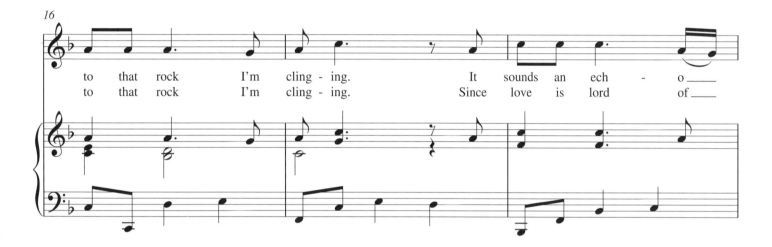

to that rock I'm cling - ing. It sounds an ech - o ____
to that rock I'm cling - ing. Since love is lord of ____

in my soul. } How can I keep from sing - ing? 2. What
Heav'n and earth, }

sing - ing?

26

un - de - filed, How can I keep from sing - ing? No storm can shake my

poco rit.

in - most calm while to that rock I'm cling - ing. ___ It

Slower

sounds an ech - o ___ in my soul. How

can I keep from sing - ing?

How happy art thou

Henry Lawes
(1596–1662)
realized by Richard Walters

How hap - py art thou and I, That
Out, out up - on those eyes, That
I'll tie my ____ heart to none,

nev - er knew how to love! ____ There's no such bless - ing
think to ____ mur - der me, ____ And he's such an ass be -
yet con - fine mine eyes, ____ But I will play my

here be - neath What - e'er there is a - bove. ____ 'Tis
lieves her fair That is not kind and free. ____ There's
game so well I'll nev - er want a prize. ____ 'Tis

lib - er - ty, 'tis lib - er - ty That ev - 'ry ____ wise man knows.
noth - ing sweet, there's noth - ing sweet To man but ____ lib - er - ty.
lib - er - ty, 'tis lib - er - ty Has made me ____ now thus wise.

Jack and Joan

Thomas Campian
(1567–1620)
realized by Richard Walters

I attempt from love's sickness to fly

from *The Indian Queen*

Henry Purcell
(1659–1695)
realized by Richard Walters

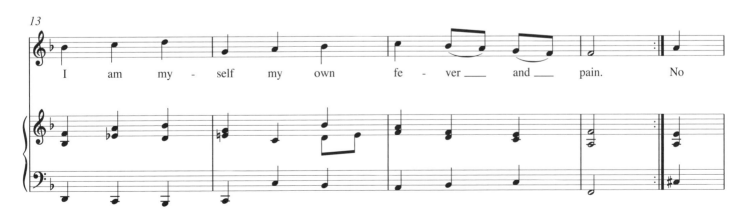

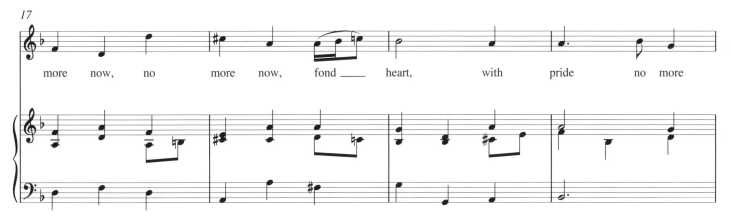

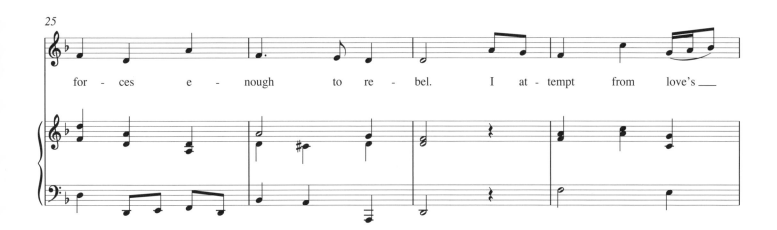

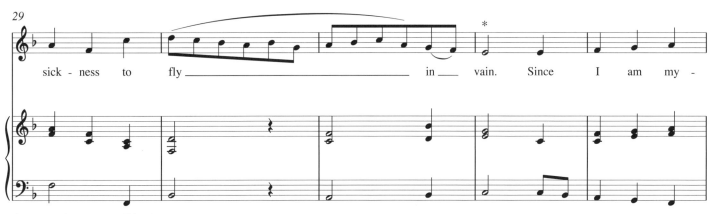

appoggiatura possible

vain. Since I am my - self my own fe - ver, since I am my

self my own fe - ver __ and __ pain. I at - tempt from love's __ sick - ness to

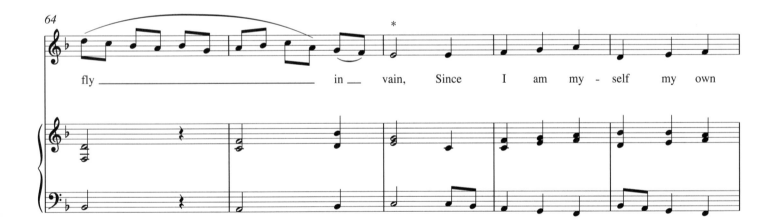

fly _____ in __ vain, Since I am my - self my own

fe - ver, since I am my - self my own fe - ver __ and __ pain.

I Gave My Love a Cherry

Mountain Song from Kentucky
arranged by Brian Dean

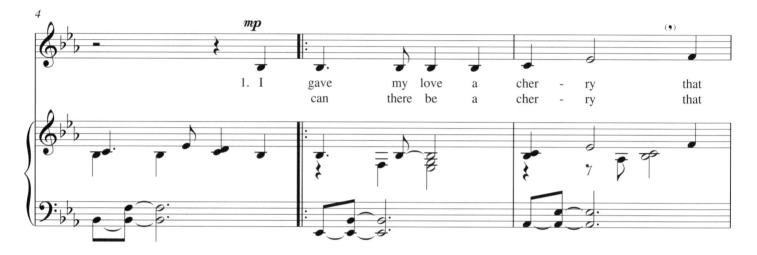

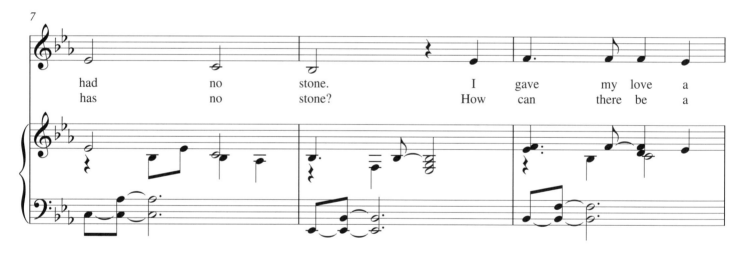

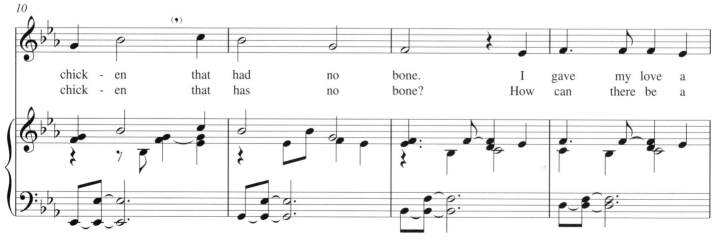

sto - ry that has no end. I
sto - ry that has no end? How

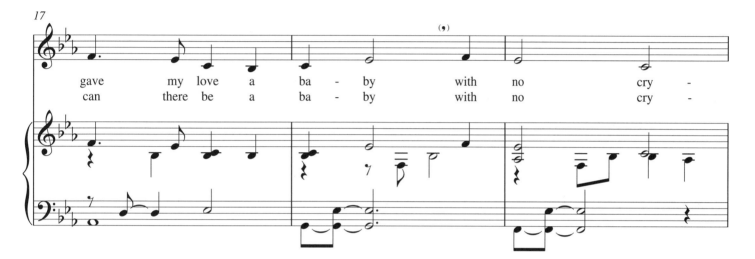

gave my love a ba - by with no cry -
can there be a ba - by with no cry -

in'.

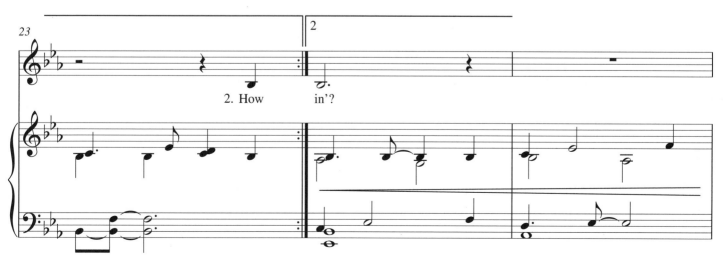

2. How in'?

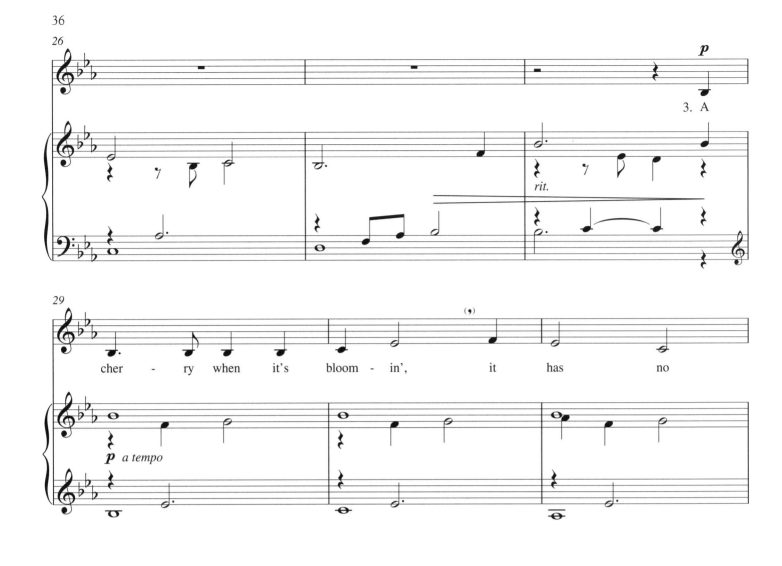

3. A

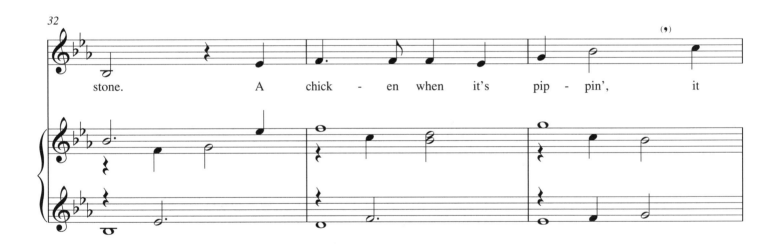

cher - ry when it's bloom - in', it has no

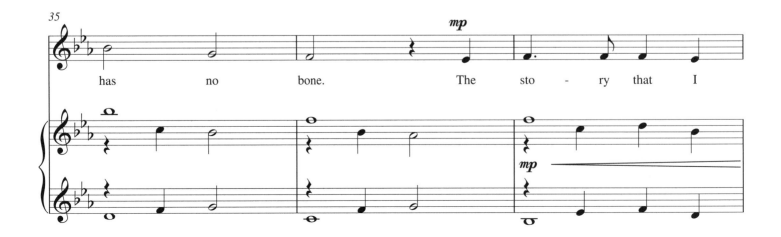

stone. A chick - en when it's pip - pin', it

has no bone. The sto - ry that I

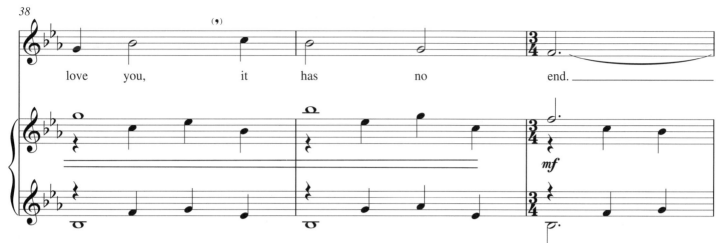

love you,   it has   no   end. _____

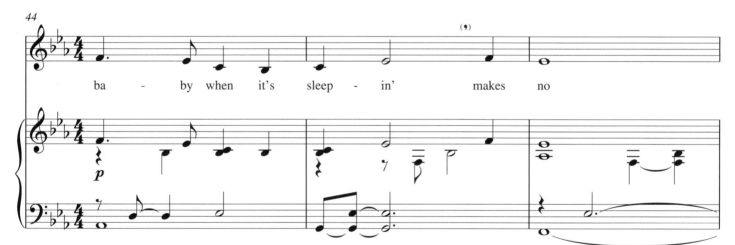

A

ba - by when it's sleep - in' makes no

cry - in'.

It was a lover and his lass

William Shakespeare
(1564–1616)
from *As You Like It*

Thomas Morley
(c. 1557–1602)
realized by Richard Walters

* *The editors' optional melodic ornamentation is for verse 2, 3 or 4. The singer may choose
to sing selected verses.*

Jacob's Ladder

African-American Spiritual
arranged by Richard Walters

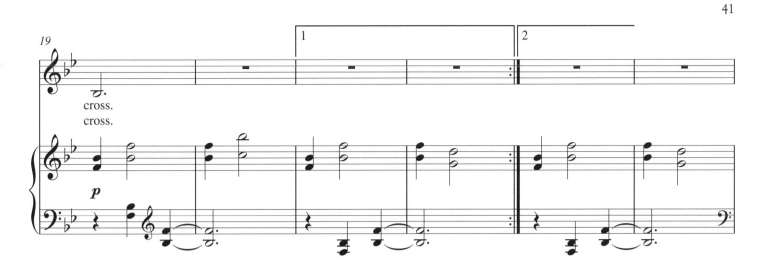

cross.
cross.

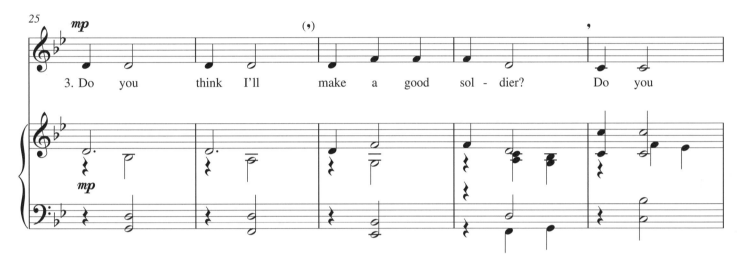

3. Do you think I'll make a good sol - dier? Do you

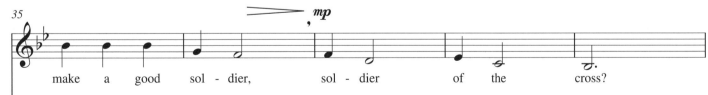
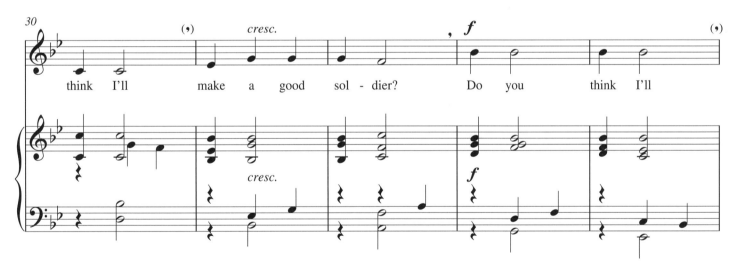

think I'll make a good sol - dier? Do you think I'll

make a good sol - dier, sol - dier of the cross?

My Lord, What a Mornin'

text based on
the Book of Revelation, 8 : 10

African-American Spiritual
arranged by Harry T. Burleigh

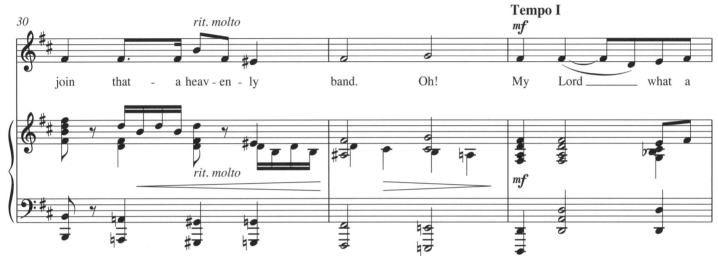

Now is the month of Maying

Thomas Morley
(c. 1557–1602)
realized by Richard Walters

The singer may choose to sing only the first two verses.

Nymphs and Shepherds

from the play *The Libertine*

Thomas Shadwell
(c. 1642–1692)

Henry Purcell
(1659–1695)
realized by Richard Walters

Flo - ra's ho - li - day, this is Flo - ra's ho - li - day, Sa - cred to

ease _____ and hap - py love, To danc - ing, to

mu - - sic, to danc - ing, to mu - - - -

- sic and to po - e - try; Your flocks may now, now, now, now, now, now,

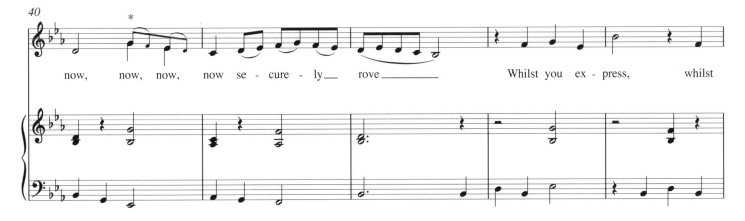

now, now, now, now se - cure - ly___ rove_____ Whilst you ex - press, whilst

you ex - press_____ your jol - li - ty.

Nymphs and Shep - herds, come_ a - way, come a - way,

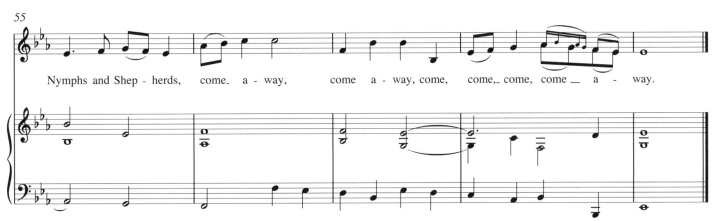

Nymphs and Shep - herds, come a - way, come_ a - way, come, come,_ come, come _ a - way.

optional melodic ornamentation by the editors

Shenandoah

19th century American Chanty
arranged by Richard Walters

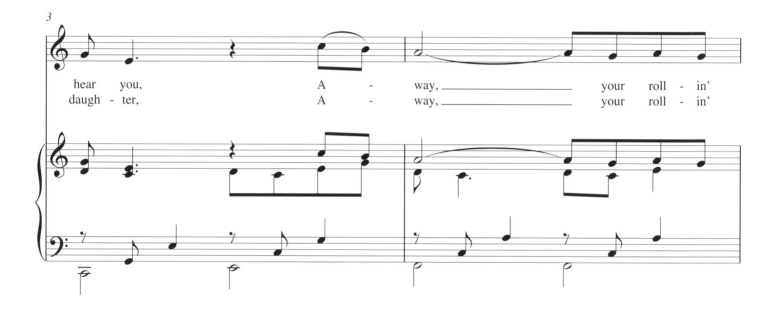

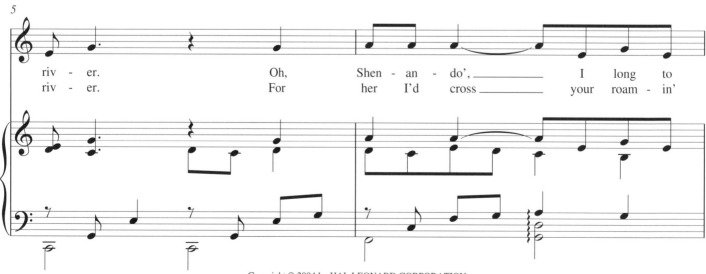

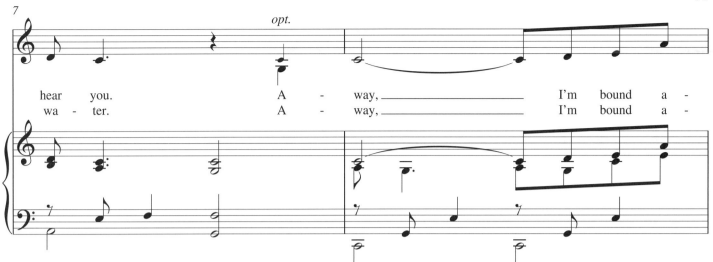

hear you. / wa - ter.   A - way,   I'm bound a-

way, / way,   'cross the wide   Mis - sou -

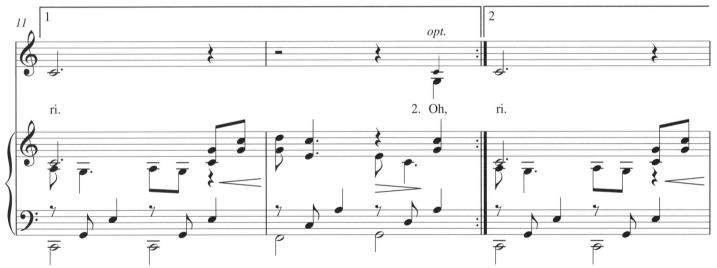

ri. / ri.   2. Oh,   ri.

3. Oh,   Shen - an - do',   I'm bound to

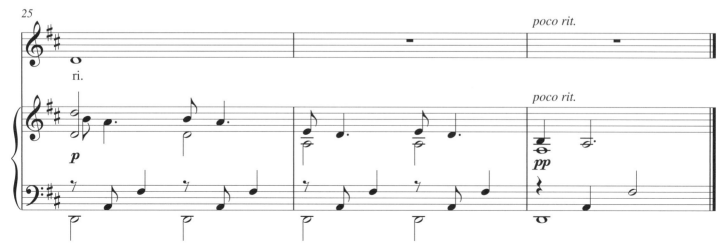

Pastime with good company

Anonymous, 16th century
attributed to King Henry VIII
realized by Richard Walters

The Silver Swan

Orlando Gibbons
(1583–1625)
realized by Richard Walters

[Slow; expressively]

last, and _ sang no more. Fare - well all joys, O

death, come close mine eyes. More geese than swans now live, more_ fools than

wise! Fare - well all joys, O death, come close mine

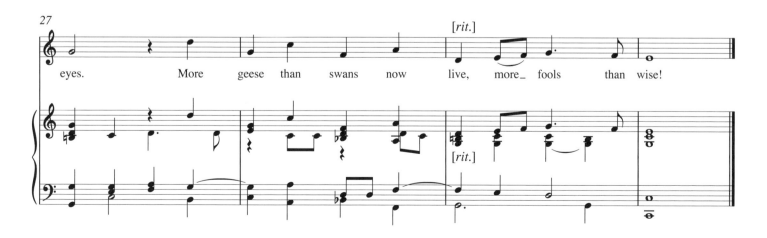

eyes. More geese than swans now live, more_ fools than wise!

[rit.]

Sometimes I Feel Like a Motherless Child

African-American Spiritual
arranged by Richard Walters

home, _____ a long way ___ from home.

Some - times I feel like I'm al - most gone, ___

some - times I feel like I'm al - most gone, ___

some - times I feel like I'm al - most gone, ___ way

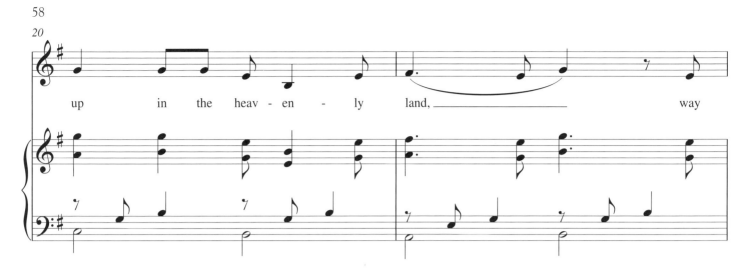

up in the heav - en - ly land, _____ way

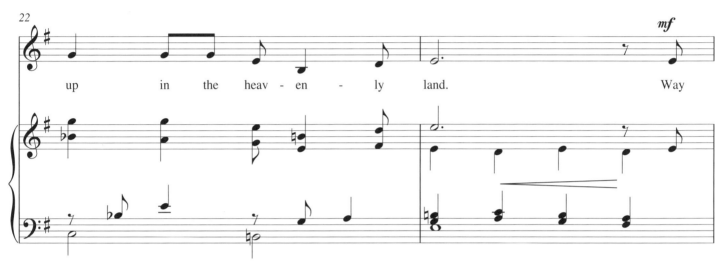

up in the heav - en - ly land. Way

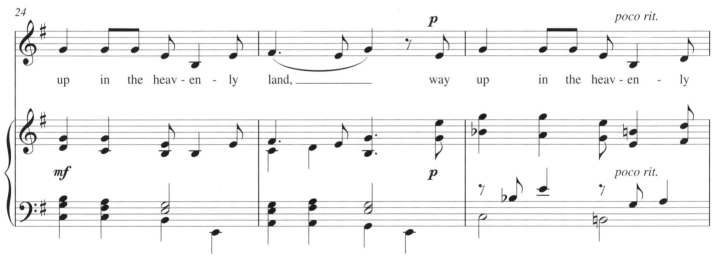

up in the heav - en - ly land, _____ way up in the heav - en - ly

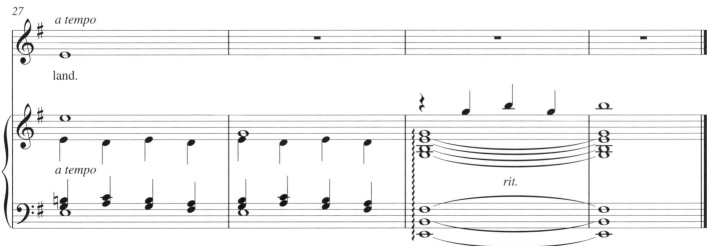

land.

Spring Sorrow

Rupert Brooke
(1887–1915)

John Ireland
(1879–1962)

Poco andante

All sud - den - ly the wind comes soft, And Spring is here a - gain; And the haw - thorn quick - ens with buds of green, And my heart with buds of

pain. My ___ heart all Win - ter lay so numb, The

poco cresc.

earth so dead and frore, That I nev - er thought ___ the

Spring would come, Or my heart wake an - y more. But

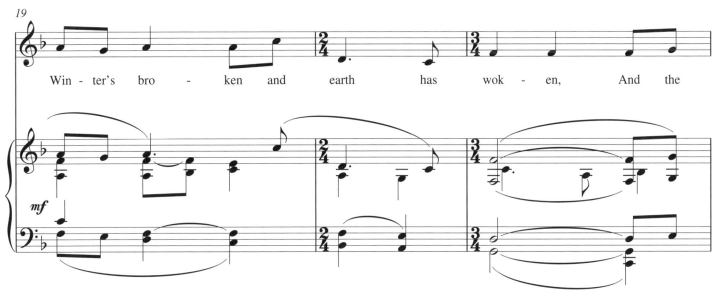

Win - ter's bro - ken and earth has wok - en, And the

small birds cry a - gain; And the haw - thorn hedge ___ puts forth its buds And my

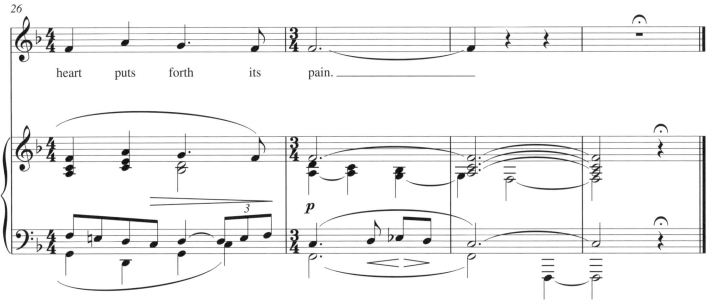

heart puts forth its pain. _____

April, 1918

This Little Light of Mine

African-American Spiritual
arranged by Christopher Ruck

All through the night, I'm gon-na let it shine,

All through the night, I'm gon-na let it shine, let it

shine, let it shine, let it shine!

Ev - 'ry - where I go,

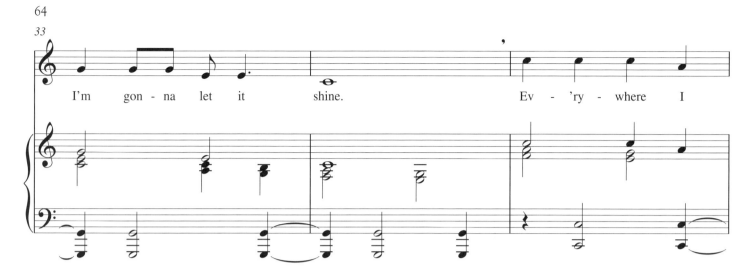

I'm gon - na let it shine. Ev - 'ry - where I

go, I'm gon - na let it shine, let it

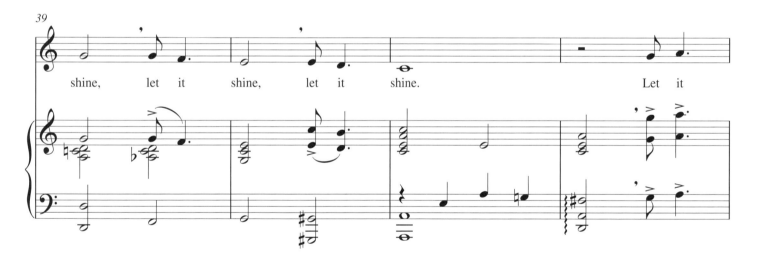

shine, let it shine, let it shine. Let it

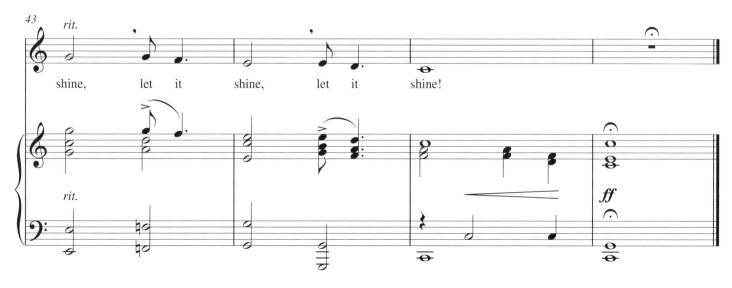

shine, let it shine, let it shine!

To the memory of my friend, Mrs. Cary-Elwes

Weep you no more

from *Seven Elizabethan Lyrics*

Anonymous

Roger Quilter
(1877–1953)

weep - ing, That now lies sleep - ing, Soft - ly now

soft - ly lies Sleep - ing, sleep - ing.

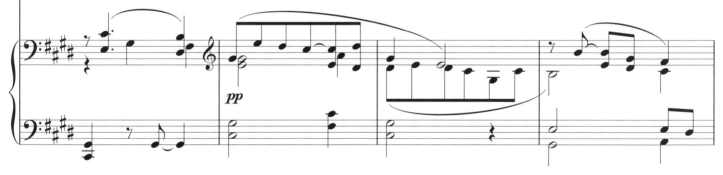

Sleep is a re-con-ci - ling, A rest that peace be-

gets; Doth not the sun rise smil - ing When

fair at even he sets? _____ Rest you, then, rest, sad eyes! Melt not in

weep - ing, While she lies sleep - ing, Soft - ly now

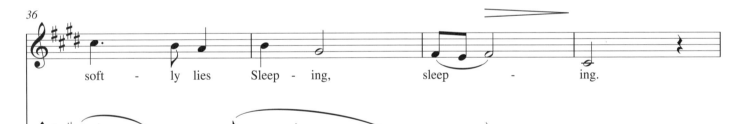

soft - ly lies Sleep - ing, sleep - ing.

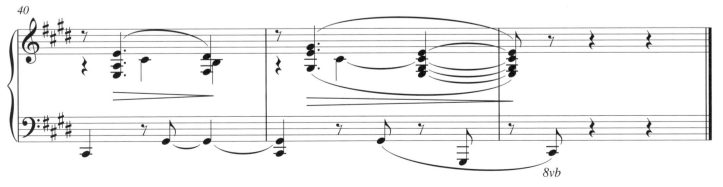

What if I never speed?

Anonymous

John Dowland
(1563-1626)
realized by Richard Walters

[Moderately]

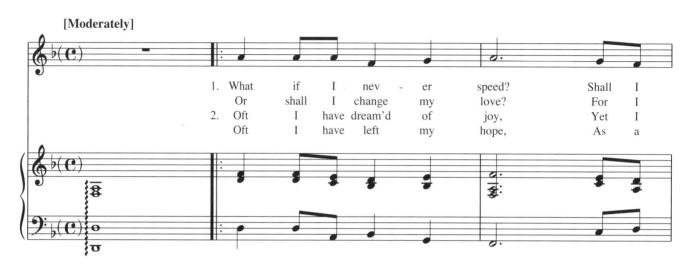

1. What if I nev-er speed? Shall I
   Or shall I change my love? For I
2. Oft I have dream'd of joy, Yet I
   Oft I have left my hope, As a

straight yield ____ to de - spair, And still on sor - row feed That ____
find pow'r ____ to de - part, And in my rea - son prove I ____
nev - er felt ____ the ____ sweet, But tired ____ with an - noy, My ____
wretch by fate ____ for - lorn, But Love aims at one scope, And ____

continue after verse 1 and verse 2

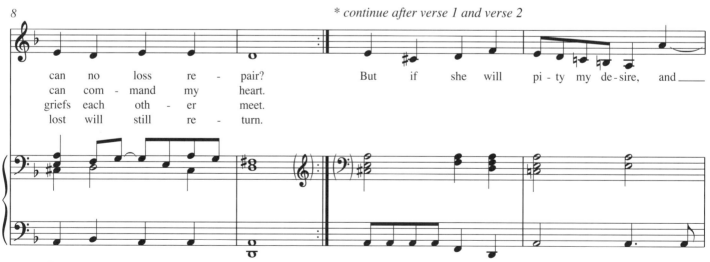

can no loss re - pair? But if she will pi - ty my de - sire, and ____
can com - mand my heart.
griefs each oth - er meet.
lost will still re - turn.

m. 10-24 may be performed twice after second verse.

___ my love re - quite, then ev - er shall she

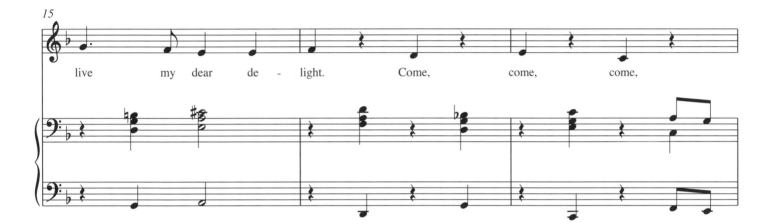

live my dear de - light. Come, come, come,

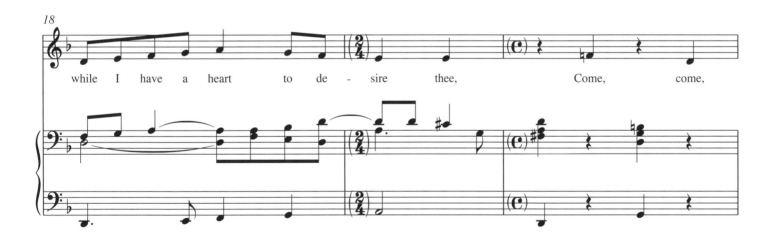

while I have a heart to de - sire thee, Come, come,

come, for eith - er I will love or ad - mire thee.

ABOUT THE ENHANCED CD

In addition to piano accompaniments playable on both your CD player and computer, this enhanced CD also includes tempo and pitch adjustment software for computer use only. This software, known as the Amazing Slow Downer, was originally created for use in pop music to allow singers and players the freedom to independently adjust both tempo and pitch elements. Because we believe there may be valuable educational use for these features in classical and theatre music, we have included this software as a tool for both the teacher and student. For quick and easy installation instructions of this software please see below.

In recording a piano accompaniment we necessarily must choose one tempo. Our choice of tempo, phrasing, ritardandos, and dynamics is carefully considered. But by the nature of recording, it is only one choice. Similar to our choice of tempo, much thought and research has gone into our choice of key for each song.

However, we encourage you to explore your own interpretive ideas, which may differ from our recordings. This new software feature allows you to adjust the tempo up and down without affecting the pitch. Likewise, the Amazing Slow Downer allows you to shift pitch up and down without affecting the tempo. We recommend that these new tempo and pitch adjustment features be used with care and insight. Ideally, you will be using these recorded accompaniments and the Amazing Slow Downer for practice only.

The audio quality may be somewhat compromised when played through the Amazing Slow Downer. This compromise in quality will not be a factor in playing the CD audio track on a normal CD player or through another audio computer program.

INSTALLATION FROM DOWNLOAD:

For Windows (XP, Vista or 7):
1. Download and save the .zip file to your hard drive.
2. Extract the .zip file.
3. Open the "ASD Lite" folder.
4. Double-click "setup.exe" to run the installer and follow the on-screen instructions.

For Macintosh (OSX 10.4 and up):
1. Download and save the .dmg file to your hard drive.
2. Double-click the .dmg file to mount the "ASD Lite" volume.
3. Double-click the "ASD Lite" volume to see its contents.
4. Drag the "ASD Lite" application into the Application folder.

INSTALLATION FROM CD:

For Windows (XP, Vista or 7):
1. Load the CD-ROM into your CD-ROM drive.
2. Open your CD-ROM drive. You should see a folder named "Amazing Slow Downer." If you only see a list of tracks, you are looking at the audio portion of the disk and most likely do not have a multi-session capable CD-ROM.
3. Open the "Amazing Slow Downer" folder.
4. Double-click "setup.exe" to install the software from the CD-ROM to your hard disk. Follow the on-screen instructions to complete installation.
5. Go to "Start," "Programs" and find the "Amazing Slow Downer Lite" application. Note: To guarantee access to the CD-ROM drive, the user should be logged in as the "Administrator."

For Macintosh (OSX 10.4 or higher):
1. Load the CD-ROM into your CD-ROM drive.
2. Double-click on the data portion of the CD-ROM (which will have the Hal Leonard icon in red and be named as the book).
3. Open the "Amazing OS X" folder.
4. Double-click the "ASD Lite" application icon to run the software from the CD-ROM, or copy this file to your hard drive and run it from there.

MINIMUM SOFTWARE REQUIREMENTS:

For Windows (XP, Vista or 7):
Pentium Processor: Windows XP, Vista, or 7; 8 MB Application RAM; 8x Multi-Session CD-ROM drive

For Macintosh (OS X 10.4 or higher):
Power Macintosh or Intel Processor; Mac OS X 10.4 or higher; MB Application RAM; 8x Multi-Session CD-ROM drive